AF574928

Why I Live in LOUISIANA

101 Dang Good Reasons

Ellen Patrick

ISBN 1-58173-291-0

Jacket and text design by Miles G. Parsons
Compiled with help from Ricky Davidson
Printed in Italy

10 9 8 7 6 5 4 3 2 1

1. Mardi Gras.

2. Hot sauce.

3. This isn't just a state, it's a separate country.

4. Children are raised to speak both Louisianan and English.

5. It's a state law that everyone over the age of 2 has to know how to fish.

6. Rockin' chairs on front porches.

7. Two kinds of Hurricanes.

8. Cayenne keeps your sinuses clear.

9. Praline-induced comas.

10. Coffee with chicory.

11. Drive-through daiquiri shops.

12. Fireworks... oh, just any old time of year.

13. Halloween in the French Quarter.

14. More parties per capita than any other state.

15. The smell of the sweet olives in spring.

16. Summer humidity eliminates need for moisturizer.

17. World headquarters for boiled food.

18. Home of the LSU Tigers.

19. Everyone can dance.

20. Everyone can cook.

21. Everyone can eat. And eat, and eat, and eat...

22. No legal penalty for eccentricity.

—∞—

23. Pirogues.

24. Swamps.

25. The Fais Do-Do.

26. No need to leave home for a taste of French culture.

—∞—

27. The "Ragin' Cajuns."

28. The Green Wave.

—∽—

29. Floodwaters provide creative opportunities for boating.

30. All roads lead to Jackson Square.

31. We got bragging rights to the longest bridge in the world.

32. Whooping cranes.

33. Pelicans.

34. Egrets.

35. Al Hirt and Pete Fountain.

36. Your basic party entertainment? Boar hunting.

—~—

37. The Bayou Bengals.

38. "Laissez les bons temps rouler."

—∞—

39. The accordion never made a comeback here—it never went away.

40. Our politicians are crooked, but at least they're honest about it.

41. The corner 7-Eleven boasts convenient selection of Voodoo dolls.

42. Visiting Catholics frequently hospitalized for shrine-overload.

43. If you ain't quite right in the head you'll fit right in.

44. No one really knows how to pronounce Natchitoches, but that's okay.

45. We're not just antebellum, we're ante-everything.

46. We got us a big ole river to keep the Mississippians out.

47. Bourbon is so popular we named our most famous street after it.

48. Beer is considered a covered dish.

49. Hospitality so intense you have to be over 21 to legally experience it.

50. When thieves steal your car, they leave a thank-you note.

51. Family is more important than fashion.

52. If you get drunk and pass out, nobody gets mad. (They are passed out, too.)

53. Home of the alligator-as-watchdog.

54. We're helping out the rest of the country by keeping an eye on Texas.

55. We're doing Yankees a favor by teaching them how to have fun.

56. Every day is a good day for a parade.

57. If you don't like the way we talk, hang around for a while. You'll sound just like us.

58. We took the best, and gave Texas and Mississippi the rest.

59. We're born knowing the secret of life: a good roux.

60. We like symphonies, as long as they have fiddles.

—m—

61. Sunday after-church pig roasts.

62. We don't need hate – we got gris gris.

63. More fortune-tellers than lawyers.

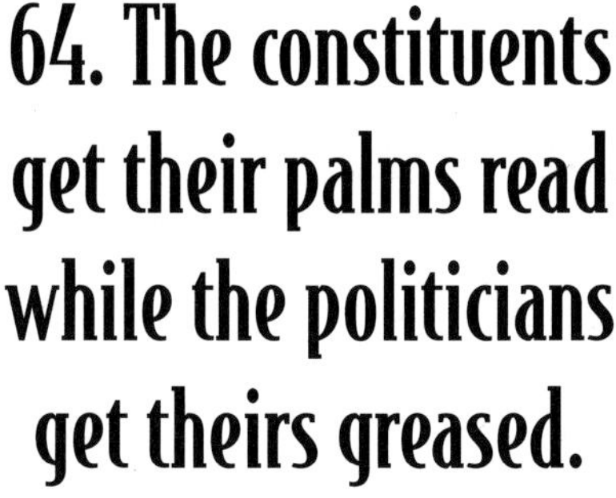

64. The constituents get their palms read while the politicians get theirs greased.

65. Dr. John isn't a physician, he's our national hero!

66. Modern dance classes are taught on table tops.

67. Fishing on the Mississippi known to induce religious visions.

68. Hey Pocky, the Neville Brothers are from here!

69. Can you say "N'Awlins"...(dawlin')?

70. Doug Kershaw.

71. Muffaletta.

72. Yats.

73. Jambalaya.

74. Around here Cher means "dear," not "Farewell Tour."

75. You think you've seen it all? You have—if you live here.

76. Filé and more filé.

77. Etouffé.

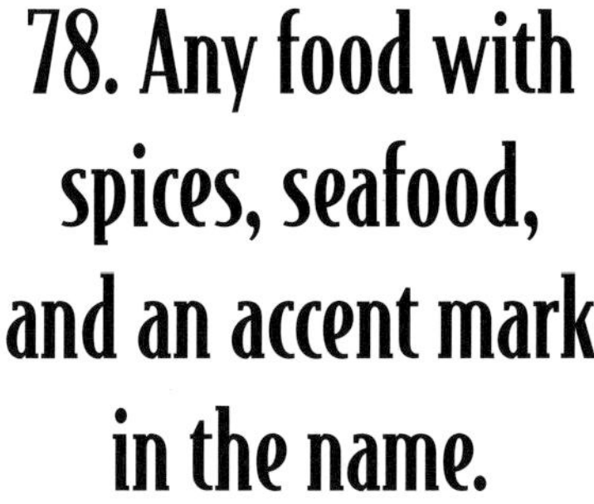

78. Any food with spices, seafood, and an accent mark in the name.

79. Lake Charles.

80. Creole cooking—widely imitated, never matched.

81. Fat City.

82. Saints in the Superdome.

83. Magnolia trees, live oaks, figs, and loquats.

84. A Pimm's Cup on a summer afternoon at the Napoleon House.

85. Show us your, um... beads.

86. Names that end in "...eaux."

87. Andouille sausage.

88. Oysters—any way you like 'em.

89. Yankees pay high prices for our old furniture.

90. Yankees pay high prices for Aunt Stella's cooking.

91. Yankees pay high prices for just about anything from our state.

92. Sunsets over the bayou.

93. Spanish moss.

94. Chewin' on sugar cane.

95. Beignets.

96. Red beans.

97. Bananas Foster.

98. Sunday brunch at Commander's Palace.

99. Home of the two-step.

100. Home of the Go-Cup.

101. You can leave Louisiana, but you'll always come home again.